A BELOVED SPECK IN THE UNIVERSE

A Beloved Speck in the Universe

Solee MacIsaac

EVERY BOOK PRESS
MMXXII

© Copyright 2022 Solee MacIsaac
All rights reserved.
ISBN: 978-0-9837714-5-6

Book Design by William Bentley
Cover Photo:
NASA/JPL-Caltech/Space Science Institute

INTRODUCTION

Thank you for giving me a second chance with more fragments of my daily perceptions put to paper, all exposed. Be kind, in perusing these short and small thoughts from my heart. The aim is to raise us up above the fray and enjoy. If you like what you read, share it with others. Happy reading, to another beloved speck in the universe.

Solee MacIsaac

*This small book is dedicated to my Usher friends,
who help sustain my aims.*

Words follow words,
Readers trace meanings,
Leaving little eyeprints.

A BELOVED SPECK
IN THE UNIVERSE

All things considered,
It is extremely lucky
We exist.

To be a beloved speck
In the Universe,
Is still pretty grand.

To reflect
On our inner worth,
  Reveals neglected fortune.

Why struggle,
When resistance
  Breeds obstacles.

  Acceptance tempers
Frustrated
  Dreams.

Life wriggles its way,
In the endless struggle
      Climbing to the light.

    Raise all the flags,
And celebrate every
      Living moment you own.

    Great is the garden,
Small is the bee,
      Wondrous to perceive both.

Love is,
Whether we partake,
Or not.

Can't like everything,
Unless you are
God.

Ever find you left your Self
Behind,
When getting ready?

Birthdays demand we
Recognize
        Time's toll.

    So precious a tiny particle
Of you,
        Joining me to my sight.

    Inner world is as large,
Or as small
        As we are.

Odd moments, not so odd.
We see,
    When we are.

    Vibrating cat whiskers
Attuned to the cosmos,
    Purring smoothly.

    Patriotism is merely
A narrow view
    Of belonging.

Politics and other strifes
Revolve around
    Misplaced responsibility.

    Art travels on currents
Of the thinnest air,
    Sparking eye lights.

    How to thank
What breathes us,
    So very lucky breath.

Give what you can,
Take little,
Receive everything.

War spawns chaos
In both directions
Of time.

What is left of you
After all dissipates
Into thinnest air?

What resides in you?
Even now,
        In this very instant?

      Speeding through ether
Never winding down,
        Perpetual planet machines.

      Are these feelings mine?
Do I own them, or are they
        Random radio bursts?

It is very clear
Life sustains
        Multiplicity not longevity.

    A day, breath, light flash,
Is it true,
        A new start at each point?

    Is reality subjective?
Pizza slices
        With various toppings?

Is there really a reality?
Or is God just
      Laughing at us?

    Flimsy at best
The firm earth
     For my feet.

    Verse = Word
UniVerse = One word
     Be.

St. Patrick!
We have more
Snakes!

Creation vs. crime
One builds, one destroys.
Maintaining balance.

Morning brightens
Night's dark fears,
Light to begin again.

Compassion
In action,
    Wordless caring.

    Examining one's motives,
A lifelong
    Study.

    Blow the bugles!
Burn the effigies,
    Finally, I exist.

    Top of the cake
Commemorating
        A single point in time.

    Painting an image
From heart to mind,
        From hands to canvas.

        From my mind to yours,
A thought
        Simply given.

How does it all work,
When we are only
    Watchers of the Play.

    Entertainment
For babes
    Streaming vividly.

    Who really benefits?
Bemoaning or applauding,
    The Play continues.

A good start
May finish last,
        But finish is the key.

    Sun's hydrogen
Shooting photons
        Of pure love.

    Earth's cycle
Refreshed,
        Spring's glory blooms.

All things flourish
In the medium of
        Encouragement.

    Hair tendrils
Erect in static air
        Signaling alertness.

    Cats.
Nature's mystery.
        Who can figure them out?

Deep deep blue,
Sky, ocean, ether,
　　The color of infinity.

One tiny speck
Too small to see
　　Receives and radiates love.

A charming smile
May disarm,
　　The guileless.

Work like you love it,
Play like it's work,
        Love always, everywhere.

    When I was a child,
I thought hands and feet terrible & beautiful.
        I still do.

    Windswept grass,
Tall and waving
        In the thunderous dusk.

Images race by,
Mind struggles to absorb,
    Too much, too much.

Graced with more
Than I deserve,
    How to thank enough?

Holding an infant
In your hands,
    So fleeting the joy.

Remembering moments
Of joy or sorrow,
        Imprints carved in heart.

    Much clamor
Yields little,
        A whisper moves oceans.

    The burning questions
Have reduced to
        Simmering surmises.

I rode on an elephant once,
Great view,
        Swaying and exciting.

    I rode on a camel once,
Got lost in sand dunes.
        I don't recommend it.

    If Love falters,
It is we who fail,
        Love is eternal, bounteous.

Omnivision Eye,
Hold my little soul
    In judgeless perspective.

Once in a lifetime,
A gleam of truth
    May shatter all lies.

Fallen tree gifts,
Last season's splendor,
    Dull and crunchy.

    Moments of togetherness
Keeps the lonely night
    From gnawing at edges.

    I saw you
From the corner of my eye.
    You were beaming halos.

    Deep within a holy place
I dwell,
    And disturb no one.

All of us rejoice,
When one of us
    Emerges.

    Listen. Tremulous notes
Quivering the strings
    Of every open heart.

    Space can't be empty.
Waves have to ride
    On something authentic.

    Sweet pinpoints of light
Can obliterate
    In proximity.

    Meetings fortuitous,
Harmonious,
    Together in a new way.

    Dig deep, climb high,
Try as hard as you can
    To reach far edge of You.

If I were a bee,
I would be enticed,
By all beautiful blossoms.

Here, in the Present,
Twinkling joy
Enlarges small soul.

Quick. Hold fast.
Darkness is creeping up,
Again.

Nerves taut, fear rising:
Listen for the high tremor.
        Ease the many into One.

    We wait.
Sometimes difficult,
        Patience secures state.

    Murderous screams in the
Night storm,
        Killer streaks, electric fire.

Calm clear morning rays,
Warm moist earth,
        Cleansed anew.

    Our tiny Earth
Fits into the setting
        Of the Milky Crown.

    Bones creak,
Muscles weaken,
        Aging is a body thing.

Crystal in its many facets
Reflects
    Many selves in one.

    Great is the world,
Infinitesimal is my fraction,
    Worlds in worlds abound.

    Lives count,
People matter,
    Even so, all is relative.

Small pebbles,
Intricate designs,
        Colors made brilliant in forest creek.

    When vision clears
The light can enter,
        Uninterrupted bliss.

    Expanse of space-time,
Immense and infinite,
        Still holds all we love.

Love to be with You always
But leaving happens
Without me.

Shopping day,
Transforming mundane into
Higher continuance.

Sweet to meet
And catch eye sparkles,
So much more than words.

Greeting friends
With your highest Self,
    Rewards both parties.

Reaping what you sow fair,
Receiving a priceless gift,
    Beyond all justice.

Slow is fine.
Hearts beat slowly at rest.
    Speed – only externally.

Love's well,
Gushing forth
Founts of purest light.

Walking, strutting, limping,
However you get there,
Home is Home.

The peak has passed,
But the fragrance lingers,
Sweet rose hangs listless.

Walking me home,
Carrying my burdens,
      No endearments trump.

    To have love, a treasure,
To give love, bestows life,
      Beloved: beyond measure.

    Put forth your best foot,
Spring into the next dance,
      Hear the true music.

Genuine help given
Is often invisible
And quiet.

Sometimes an inward
Glimpse
Can spot faulty motives.

Crying isn't unmanly,
Just an orb cleansing
Of faulty vision.

Whitest light emblazons
Sacred dome
      Of unearthly perception.

    All who enter here,
Leave themselves
      Behind.

    Death after life,
Although expected,
      Nothing like Death in life.

Stars peeking through
A mask of shadows,
Inspire me to do the same.

Gems can instruct
If one listens
To their inner hearts.

Diamonds result
From infinite payment
And transformation.

To be simple, concise, substantive,
Is work.
        Flowing length is easy.

    Days stream by,
While moments loom large
        And stick much better.

    Weeping skies,
Abundant drinks
        Quench scratchy throats.

Long drive in the sun,
Destination
 Realized at last.

Contacting sublime:
Beautiful, sending it forth:
The pinnacle.

Stomach wants fed,
Mouth wants taste,
 Heart wants peace.

Variety of wants,
Satisfaction
       Is only temporary.

    Wandering through
Spring daffodils, thinking,
       The world could do worse.

    Prone and positive
Watching reforming clouds,
       A good blue-white view.

Hang on too tight,
You may lose.
        Everything has to breathe.

    Although busy,
It seems a slow day,
        Perhaps impatience rises.

    Anticipation can trick
Us into believing
        Outcomes are knowable.

A goodly amount of pleasure
Comes from
        The most simple.

    Numbers can tell a lot,
Some things not so good,
        Like on my scale.

    Finding You once again,
I was misplaced,
        Never You.

Doctors found a speck
Next to my optic nerve,
    I am sure You put it there.

This beloved speck in the
Universe
    Is grateful to all.

The best is when there is
No you or me,
    Only the utter light.

The global Earth
Spins, soars, spirals,
        In endless Sun's song.

    Can you hear?
Softest sweetest sound:
        Souls free from Earth's pull.

    Older beings need meds,
Even non-humans;
        Maintenance increases.

We shelter in each other,
We the pillars,
    Lift up our sacred structure.

Mouth the words
That tell your truth,
    No one hears but the brave.

Buy your ticket,
Take the ride,
    Committing is everything.

It is only March,
The hot sun is preparing
    For the brutal summer.

Coolness will be
At a high premium,
    Fans, ice, gauzy wear.

Predicting can be risky,
When you are right –
    Momentous.

Lay down your weapons,
Remove your armor,
 Be who you are at last.

Trees can be close
In their entangled embrace,
 There is sky for everyone.

Slow growth is best,
Rushing inhibits
 Correct completion.

One thing at a time,
One moment is enough
    For increment of change.

    Chickens cackling,
Eggs hatching,
    Life continues.

    Our world seems large,
Then small,
    Size is so arbitrary.

A blank page
Can be intimidating,
    Challenging, or inviting.

Writer's block
Is fear of innocent
    Blank pages.

An abundance of fruit
In rainbow colors
    Feels like wealth, security.

Fitting in,
Is not as important,
    As following the right way.

    Followers recognize
A creative
    Soul.

    Modesty and grace
Encircle a quiet
    Heart.

Beauty captures eyes
And hearts; but fades,
    Except in eternity.

The year's bounty
Condensed and revisited,
    Fodder for Springing forth.

Fashion – personal style –
Before or after its time:
    Is discordant.

Integration takes time,
Effort, and correct energy,
        To make perfect anything.

    Nature serves old Earth,
In an effortless act
        Of endless Love.

    Concentrated attention,
Applied effort, isn't work,
        Unless you don't want to do it.

Accomplishment,
Regardless,
 Builds will and being.

Sometimes it feels
Like I am barely able
 To catch up with my Self.

 Halting inner momentums
Can give amazing
 Perspectives.

Mastering art forms takes
A lifetime of inspiration,
    Effort and Love.

    Presence flashes on-off,
Like glass shards hanging
    In windy sunlight.

    Soft light sneaking
Through the blinds
    Wakes my sleepy form.

Family shores up
My flagging enthusiasm
With beams of rosy joy.

Our cherished planet
Suffers from our
Mistreatment and neglect.

Readers are so important,
Lest the words drop off
Into an abyss of unread.

Short and sharp is not
Simple:
        Terse can be cruel.

    Simplicity is
Condensed, specific,
        Pure: like You.

    Around the circle
One more time.
        Will I learn this time?

To the doctor,
Things not going so well,
Again.

Balance attained,
But never for long,
Difficult to stay in tune.

Summer winds
Blowing through my mind,
It won't be long, now.

Reaching for a golden ring,
Just able to touch it,
    Foiled once more.

    If I could be good as I wish,
All would be well,
    Or so I think.

    Work begets work;
If you don't think so,
    Try cleaning your closet.

Being small helps,
Autonomy provides
Room to grow undisturbed.

Heart poor,
Is a tragic
Way to live.

Music: beautiful language,
All can understand,
What needs no words.

Being surly doesn't help
Accomplishing.
        Only right attitude helps.

    Our wealth stems
From the sacred space
        Full of pure light.

    Come to the bazaar,
Take my armful
        Of fresh flowers.

Warm your heart
Near the fire
    Of my longing.

    Love stretches between
Your needs
    And other's needs.

    Graceful is the action
Of the lover,
    Never resentful.

I live,
Breathe,
      Love.

    Walk with me
To the edge
    Of each other.

    Clarity of purpose
Can reduce error
    And lead to success.

Small efforts
Are only small
    To those who are practiced.

Who gave permission
To that unhappy voice
    Burbling from my throat?

Surface is smooth,
What lies beneath?
    You, find a way to reveal.

Tiny hurts
Release
    My patience in a burst.

    White and round
Is the moon face
    Smiling at the night tulips.

    Conscience overwhelms
Unbridled cacophony
    With silence.

Being open,
To new concepts,
May be worth the risk.

No one who eats mice
Is that wise,
Including owls.

Suffering is unpleasant,
A good attitude can soften
The blows.

Dark encasing the light,
Our bodies,
        Sometimes leak brilliance.

    Little kisses rest easily,
Smoothing
        My furrowed brow.

    Let those who judge you,
Carry their burden
        Of judgement, alone.

Private life,
A treasured illusion,
Necessary at times.

Shift perspective
To gain
New insight.

The length of the road
Isn't as important
As where it leads.

Hearts cry out
For the nourishment
    Of love.

    The only way to have love
Is to continually
    Give love.

    Character means:
One has suffered
    And overcome.

If I were a flea,
An ant could be
Very imposing.

If more is less,
Why do we always
Want more?

Our limitations
Make it difficult
To know our true position.

Change is.
We are change.
        Stopping is death.

    Eternity is not static.
Infinity is not long.
        The present is all there is.

    Green is back.
Trees are happily waving
        Their new Spring attire.

Small farms define their
Growing spaces,
    And dot land with charm.

Looking down
On our living place,
    Seeing how small we are.

The divine arch
Within,
    Shelters our precious soul.

Eye of light
Feeds
        Our spiritual growth.

    Our baby self
Learned by trying,
        Same for us now.

    Doors of our head
Allow good things
        To enter, not exit.

There is comfort
In gatherings,
    Many beings sharing joy.

Books are ever giving
Friends
    Who help our hearts open.

Attempting to be the same
Inside and out,
    Can be challenging.

Slanting rays
Of morning
    Greet my sleepy lids.

    Everything needs our
Attention
    Lest entropy wins.

    Each day,
Another step,
    On the way to completion.

Wondering what cats do,
When not interacting
With us humans.

Sheer explosion of Spring
Growth, color, fragrance,
Is overwhelming.

Beauty, variety, abundance
Of surface impressions,
Conceal inner meanings.

To look deep into this world
Requires looking
    Deep into ourselves.

    Understanding,
Standing under,
    Is a great key.

    To be small, simple, quiet,
Unobtrusive,
    And see everything, is all.

>What is best in us
Is usually
>Quiet.

>Your truth, my truth,
Real Truth
>Is hard to come by.

>Mindfulness
Is really mindlessness,
>The empty is the full.

Even when harsh,
The light
    Is the aim.

Alive is moveable, flexible,
Dead is stiff, hard.
    The same for psychology.

They who are difficult
Are most in need
    Of kindness.

Harboring slights
Can inhibit compassion
And forgiveness.

The days and hours
Stretch
When waiting.

If you can't be with Love,
Decorate the halls
In anticipation.

State-driven joys
  Light up the world
      In sacred harmony.

     Rain returns,
  Green turns neon,
      Tulips open.

    Nature and heaven
  Blend their grace
      To decorate Earth.

Freedom is a state
Not related
    To circumstance.

Cradle the nubile
In two hands.
    Young mature very fast.

Minds fill up,
Sweep all away.
    Retrieve clear eyes, heart.

The heartless one
Stays in shadows,
        Pulling strings with glee.

    The shining one
Quells all shadows
        And sees Truth.

    Change of scene
Can sometimes
        Stimulate new efforts.

Familiarity can be
Too comfortable,
  Inducing sleepy thoughts.

Clasp hands,
Entwine fingers, closeness
  Engenders stronger bonds.

Water, giver of life,
Falls from the sky.
  No charge.

So much wealth
Is free.
        Except money.

    Silence,
Now and then,
        Keeps us sane.

    Alarm bells, sirens,
Help to remind
        The need to Be.

The arched white bridge:
Supports anchored low,
 Pillars soar high over bay.

Inside out myself,
A dear one
 Is in trouble.

Challenges
Can break us,
 But only to let in more light.

Even sad memories
Can tempt one
    And interrupt the Light.

    Stretch out your arms,
Enfold the empty,
    Draw it into your very core.

    Empty space
Filled with light,
    Is all You need.

Landscapes streaming by,
Sun and shadow
    Altering views, of color.

Rooftops,
Extremely tall buildings,
    Big city sights and sounds.

A country girl
Gaping
    Like a child.

Feeling ashamed
Isn't bad,
        But a chance to see Truth.

    They prick us with their
Sword tips,
        To keep us awake.

    Prison isn't all there is,
The gates
        Are wide open.

>   Fertility of mind,
Can be
>   Weed growth.

>   This day is almost over,
Have I earned
>   More being today?

>   Long waiting,
Tedious,
>   Earning patience.

Drinking deeply
Of the pure water,
        Feeling its long journey.

    A kiss, a promise,
An anchor for the future
        To grow upon.

    Sheets of gray rain
Melting everything
        Into meaningless similarity.

Even cities
Have to bathe,
    To achieve freshness.

A parting,
Long thoughts,
    Long waiting to rejoin.

Best thing about hospitals,
They are clean, helpful,
    But you still feel smothered.

Friends supply
The needed
    Bolstering and truth telling.

    Hammers, eggbeaters,
Having the right tool
    Is half the job.

    Being trustworthy
Is an honor and a privilege,
    As is trusting.

Betraying trust
Belies a lack of honor
And valuation.

We get to see new moon,
But not new Earth,
Unless we are in space.

We drop into our lives
And everything is all here,
We don't see beginnings.

Church, temple, mosque,
A holy place for Self,
    Is within, not without.

    Spring clean your
Inner house
    'Til it sparkles.

    Sacrifice being clever
For the higher state
    Of sincere Not-Knowing.

Skyscrapers, bridges,
Loud sounds, brash sights:
    Have a warm hand to hold.

Experiences vary
In intensity and value
    Making us dimensional.

On the shrouded bay
Foghorn sounds mournful,
    But can guide the blind.

Weeds are climbing,
Before dry and gold,
      Set the cows to chomping.

    Discard all that is
Unnecessary.
      Good practice for dying.

    A small kindness
Could be large
      In someone's world.

Watching the light change,
Wondering,
Was love with me this day?

Sleeping people
Drive, eat, work, play, suffer
For the wrong reasons.

Formality can seem fake,
Or it can help remind us
Who we really are.

Mountains, valleys, rivers,
Forests, meadows, bays,
    Earth provides, we reside.

    Pick up that sock,
Empty the refuse,
    It may be your only chance.

    New shoes,
New clothes,
    Same me.

Giving generously
Feels like receiving.
    Things are upside down.

We often ride the joy wave,
Not noticing the ocean
    Of support beneath us.

Clouds around the Sun
Are near to us –
    Higher up, Sun shines clear.

Sun has his being in space
Far from other beings.
    Must be lonely.

    Greet each person
With warmth and cheer,
    Seeing again unknown.

    People connect casually,
Deeper friendship
    Must be earned.

Grace in speech,
Grace in manner,
      Wins over physical beauty.

    Please and thank you
Can take you a long way,
      But only if really meant.

    Don't be afraid of unknown,
Really most we know
      Is wrong anyway.

Having the right scale,
One can step between
        Wrong choices.

    A block of wood
Is only that,
        Unless in sculptor's hands.

    To see beyond oneself
A great achievement,
        Waking up lights the terrain.

Lightning strikes
Are too infrequent
To stay shocked awake.

Building a ladder to God
Is good,
Not climbing is a mistake.

True words
Come from above
The mind.

Our inner light
Shines on eternity,
    Where it was born.

Thoughts live in a garden;
Some are plucked, saved.
    Others, weeds: composted.

Green thumbs
Nourish growth and
    Harmonize Nature's gifts.

Desires focused correctly
Can bring us to doorstep,
Only desireless can enter.

Is it not strange
Our world is surrounded
By empty space?

Almost as if
We are the many thoughts
In Earth's head.

Sweet the sound of
Flute's mystery.
    Is it answers we seek?

Answers are like
Open windows.
    Are we inside or outside?

Solutions are practical
Answers,
    Useful for accomplishment.

Some answers
Lead
To more questions.

Accepting what comes
Is to be truly grateful
For the gift of life.

Graciousness and humility
Win hearts,
Progress steadily.

From roots to treetops
Majestic oaks stand firm,
        Sheltering smaller critters.

    The Moon is a crescent,
Again,
        New plantings, reapings.

    Pupils expand to take in
A sea of tulips,
        Colors awash in dew.

Earth's light is golden.
Divine light is a colorless
  Blaze of wakefulness.

Compliments and the like
Are, at times, more difficult
  To receive than to give.

Fine music
Can elevate souls
  To higher realms.

The beauty of a note is
Determined by those
    Surrounding it.

    It is a wondrous feeling
To be a beloved
    Speck in the universe.

    Straining to hear
My beating heart
    Amidst cosmos of stars.

Hit the brakes!
A family of asteroids
    Is crossing your path.

Speeding through galaxy
One must see some
    Strange formations.

To be a small moon
Of a mighty planet,
    What sights may there be.

Rings upon rings,
Colored lights,
       Smoke, fire – explosions.

    Earth and her prisms
Are delight enough
       Until that journey appears.

    Quiet evenings together
Is a blessing
       That I cherish.

My mother used to say:
Small feet signify beauty;
 She had small feet.

From elephant to mole
One's size is relative to
 One's living space.

Potential life:
Eggs,
 And good for breakfast too.

Sweet C-Lover,
Many friends,
        Love and nourishment.

    Haircut,
Clean and simple,
        Fresh look.

    New leaves,
Regrowth neon green,
        Trees grateful for Spring.

Slow moving river,
Bending and meandering
    Home to the wide ocean.

Wide white magnolia
Blossom,
    Who fashioned you?

Our Sun not so large
In the garden of stars.
    To us it blossoms immense.

Great is the need
For sustenance,
        Both physical and spiritual.

    Divine light
Graciously descends,
        To the incredibly lucky.

    Spending my time
With You
        Is no time at all.

Country living has its drawbacks,
But dwelling in Nature
A great privilege.

Serve the people wisely,
All are troubled,
Just like you.

Kings and beggars
Have a role to play;
Play yours with gratitude.

If the shoes are too big
Try to wear them anyway;
      Grow into your larger Self.

    Behave as if you are
As good as
      You wish to be.

    It is not so far now,
The light guides me
      To my celestial home.

Angel challenging me –
You work hard,
    Yet love unconditionally.

Feeling low,
Antenna's up!
    Catch a high beam.

Swells of music can
Carry us to places
    Of sublime remembering.

Discrimination
Is not negative,
    But a quality endorser.

    Washing someone's
Dishes
    Is a sweet gift.

    No matter how far apart,
Love stretches between,
    Sending subtle messages.

Peer pressure
Can drive us
    Where we don't want to go.

Up the mountain, swiftly –
Catch a rainbow
    On your thumb.

How much have I invested
In my Self today?
    Or have I relied upon past efforts.

Morning streams forth
Raising flagging thoughts
        To You, present: awake.

        White, the colorless color,
Of purest light,
        From above the dark sea.

     Solid and strong
My inner conviction,
        Pulled, scored by ruffians.

You keep my best safe;
My incrementally growing
   Treasure.

Create, build, provide,
Strong impulses in
   Humans, ants, birds, bees.

Making an error
Is normal,
   Admitting it, less so.

Tender feelings
Caressing our hearts
        Reveal deep compassion.

    Like Cinderella,
You fit nicely into
        Your clear glass stance.

    World news
Isn't very new,
        Same old world.

Pampas grass, foxtails,
Ostrich plumes:
    Fluffy and gorgeous.

Little breezes
Bring fragrances,
    Traces of jonquils, tulips.

You can hide,
But not
    From your Self.

Pan for gold,
Filter the most cherished
      From all the rabble.

    Hills and valleys,
Streams and meadows,
      Nature's civilization.

    Greet each moment
With your true Self,
      No time for pretense.

Milky sky
Dropping finches
    On my porch bannister.

Palomino horses
Grazing under
    Flowering apple trees.

Pink blossom-speckled
Walkway
    Ascending rock garden.

Dreams aligned,
Working together,
        Doubly blessed.

      Mist rising from the ground
In foggy tendrils,
        Obscuring dripping forest.

    Non-verbal
Communication
      Is sometimes best.

Essence and glee
Go together like
        Presence and silence.

    Accolades for all attaining
Their heart's desire,
        Even more for keeping it.

    Master an art form,
Phenomenal,
        Master self, incomparable.

Let the daily grind
Be your coffee,
        Not your way of life.

    Each obstacle surmounted
Is worthy of celebration
        On the way to completion.

    Take a walk,
Discover
        The season's offerings.

Genuflect to all who
Love the Light.
    Bathe in it regularly.

    Small beings with tails, fur,
Can be a joy
    Or a royal nuisance.

    Crank up the energy
And dance 'til you
    Drop all unnecessary.

Vacations are only fun
If you leave yourself
        Behind.

    Go with the dawn Light,
Swiftly move through our
        Galaxy to the in-between.

    Our neighboring galaxy
Is a thought away.
        Call first.

Deep caring
For a convalescent
   Is love in action.

The theater of friends
Is lucky abundance
   We don't take for granted.

Many drops make ocean,
Humanity's being would
   Make a colorful person.

Cows grazing, standing,
Reclining, munching grass.
    Cows.

    First light,
Tremulous,
    Slips beneath sleepy lids.

    We benefit from so many
Lucky things, it is difficult
    To be grateful enough.

We learn by experience,
But real Knowing
   Is a different category.

Listening to the sounds,
Tempo of our day,
   Feeding directly to heart.

Give me a big sombrero
To shield my fragile self
   From blazing solar glare.

Carry her books,
Value every moment together;
    Over too soon.

    Remember to look
Behind the scenes,
    That is most interesting.

    Outer space is an enigma,
But then,
    So is inner space.

The realm of angels
Can't be inner or outer,
    Must have its own domain.

Neighboring countries,
Like big and small siblings,
    Can squabble over rights.

No one can really own
Planet Earth,
    But illusions persist.

Watching self say things
I don't know to be true,
        Causes cringing inside.

        Steeped in the well of truth,
A lie
        Alarms many levels.

    Easter eggs,
Chocolate bunnies,
        Cutesie fertility traditions.

Light a candle,
Light ten,
 Every small light reminds.

 Soaring steeple and spire,
Reaching for heaven,
 Physical symbol of spirit.

 Shelter, food, air and water,
We take for granted,
 Lucky us. Yet still we crave.

Our true communication
Is more on the soul level
        Rather than our brain's.

    Things aren't colors seen,
All reflect a color not
        Part of them. Nature's trick.

    Subjectivity isn't bad
As long as
        You recognize it.

Doing more
Than you want to do,
    Sometimes feels satisfying.

Compromise is strength.
Your own way
    Can be limiting.

Littering is a way
Of disrespecting
    Humans and Nature.

When I was a child,
I used to dream I was
    Climbing a ladder to the sky.

Our sky actually ends
At the edge of space,
    Where dreams begin.

Musical instruments
In the right hands
    Can change inner states.

What is it to evolve?
Invisible change to
    Inner freedom.

Birds chirping dawn song
Opens the day
    To new possibilities.

What a pleasure
Hearing and seeing,
    There is so much.

Our senses, a joy, a trial,
Seeing, hearing,
        Hopefully not believing.

    What makes you, You?
Is a drop so different
        From the ocean?

    Reading my own thoughts,
Wondering,
        Whose are they, really?

Fairytales can have
Happy endings;
   Reality – hit or miss.

Good fortune, bad fortune,
Both attach us
   To the illusion of this world.

Heaven rains down
Good and bad,
   We have to discriminate.

Rough times,
Smooth times,
        Find the middle, inside.

    Mystical eyes,
What does my cat see?
        He just won't tell me.

    If no expectations,
Whatever happens
        Can be a great discovery.

Is there a shred
Of recognizable me,
    That lives beyond death?

The obstacle of me
Gets in my way,
    And blocks perfect Light.

Imagination:
The default
    In the machine.

Walking on the street,
Seeing little, swimming
    In a lake of dreams.

    Acting as if
All is real,
    Even myself.

    Sons and daughters
Appear from you,
    Then disappear from you.

Home is comforting,
But only temporarily
On the way to real Home.

Losing weight,
Is an act of
Patience.

Bright yellow-green leaves
Are glistening
In Spring sunshine.

Even if pathway is dark,
Take my arm, walk together
Toward the Light.

Subtleties in relationships
Bring closeness,
Or distance.

The third point,
Which helps both,
Is yearning for the Light.

Earth's globe is big, small,
Depending who's looking,
And from where.

Youth is about what
To do first, and boredom.
Aging: about maintenance.

Sometimes I forget
How very special it is,
To be given this life.

Make center meaningful,
Lest you spin
    Like a wobbly top.

    Our moon is an anchor
To keep us tethered,
    And secure Earth's wobble.

    Striving for virtue
Is excellent exercise.
    Failure is one ladder rung.

A Beloved Speck in the Universe

Smiling even when alone,
Lifts your outlook
Instantly.

A laughing infant
Sparkles like a
Burbling brook.

Throw your head back,
Raise arms to night's sky,
Envelop the mighty stars.

This world is fascinating,
But it is not
    All there is.

    Fix your inner eye
On the invisible
    Truth.

    Craving, grasping,
Is desperation, not
    Acceptance or patience.

Trust in a worthy goal
Motivates
 Small efforts.

Classic isn't old,
It is ageless,
 Like You.

Opposites are linked,
And can teach us
 Moderation.

Good performers reveal
Their inner selves
      Through their art forms.

    Courage is a curious
Aspect that engenders
      Acclaim or is invisible.

    Line of cars
Stopped in the road,
      For hen and nine chicks.

Rain so precious,
For the dry ground,
    Lilies open their throats.

Dark times
Can prove challenging,
    If can't transform, endure.

The age old adage:
Things change,
    Is perpetually true.

Summer months ahead
Summoning joy and fear,
    Foreboding wildfires.

    Our chance at loving
Is everyone
    We know.

    Coming together,
With open hearts,
    Sharing our best Selves.

Be aware of awareness,
See your seeing,
It only takes Light.

Blue-black clouds,
Emptying themselves
Over all asunder.

Civilization
Isn't always civil,
But buildings can be pretty.

Wary cat at doorstep
Does not trust
    Errant weather.

    Good things, bad things arrive
Unannounced at our door.
    Our job: decide who enters.

    Beautiful landscapes
Lift our hearts,
    Turn our thoughts upward.

Pray for a larger capacity
To endure, to be grateful.
All things are temporary.

A crowning wreathe
Of sweet clover,
Adorns Spring nymphs.

Cool blue pond
Amidst the green hills:
A drink for wooly sheep.

Seas of waving tulips
Bow as I pass,
      On this path of high honor.

    A grand march
To the water's edge,
      Mother and ducklings.

    Apple spice muffins
Very popular,
      Smells really inviting.

Inner quiet,
Provides a space to
Actually live.

Memory is an odd
Kind of life outside of life,
Fluid and changeable.

Energy that initiates
Can be raucous,
Changing status quo.

Whirling dervish
Streams celestial strands
      Round spiral of existence.

    Cozy cat
Warming fur
      Next to fireplace.

    Bestow your precious
Attention
      In two directions.

A Beloved Speck in the Universe

Do not take for granted
That you are in the
Picture.

Never underestimate
The value
Of your Self.

Valuation,
A necessity for
Prioritizing.

Wood fires
Warm noses, toes,
      And chilled cats.

    The margin
Of the circle
    Is all there is.

    The empty
Is the full
    In right order.

    Many hands build,
One mind
      Designs.

    Lend your strength
To a holy work,
      Your own Presence.

    The dome of light
Above and in you,
      Shields and enriches.

Great is the need,
Greater is the supply
    Of divine Love.

Spread your
Budding wings,
    Lift yourself to the Sun.

It is not for us
To understand everything,
    But serve higher purpose.

To be open to learning
And to actually learn,
Are wonderful things.

It is difficult to learn the new;
If there is no room for it,
Let go of the old first.

A chime, a gong, a bell,
Reverberates in our heart,
If we allow it.

Ears-heart, eyes-mind,
Touch-body; senses,
        Hooks to the world.

    Intentionally doing
Is so different,
        Than just being efficient.

    Carrying wood to fireplace,
Securing logs into fire,
        Being here.

Smattering of rain on roof,
Cat's eyes straight up,
        What does this forebode?

    Many flowers,
Much fragrance,
        Many colorful walkways.

    Moments
Stretch or shrink
        With our desires.

Layers upon layers
Of patterns
        Compose life's pathway.

    Some experiences
Are difficult to digest,
        Time is required.

    Jumping levels
Demands heroic efforts:
        Negative to positive.

The closer we come
To that which is sought,
    Difficulties increase.

Years in
We think we know,
    Must relinquish knowing.

    Allow yourself to be wrong,
Acknowledge it,
    Pathway opens.

Setbacks can be viewed
As opportunities to
      Reassess the aim.

    Wet shoes, wet hair,
Puddles
      Adorn my driveway.

    Grind your teeth, grimace,
Makes no difference
      To the outcome.

Funny how we approach
Controlling things,
    Better to control ourselves.

Pale gray sky frames
Glowing
    Yellow-green maple.

Lush and moist
Kind of day,
    Sweetening my mood.

Some think forcing works,
Others use passivity,
    Formulas aren't for us.

    Discernment, though necessary,
Can create
    Illusion of control.

    Detachment is not
Lack of caring,
    But lack of identification.

Eating lighter and simpler,
Fuels bodies and minds,
With high octane.

Let complications reside
In beautiful patterns,
Not in our hearts.

Being truly gracious
Is rare,
Taking credit, the norm.

Delight to see a friend
Unexpectedly,
    Gift from above.

    Pleasure of connection
Links hearts
    In a high moment.

    Staying on the right path
Is a lifetime aim,
    Worthy of the attempt.

Surface of life is elaborate,
Difficult to find a crack
　　To slip inside and see.

Quoting ancient sages
Isn't plagiarism or copying,
　　Just good sense.

Being playful
Can lift
　　Sour moods.

Finding a key to happiness
Not as good as the key
      To realizing sleep.

    Good Friday
Is more than good
      For all who Love.

    Deep shadows
Just accentuate
      The brightest light.

Reasons, like answers,
Are not always
　　Immediately available.

New books
Are like friends
　　You haven't met yet.

Unravel the mysteries
Of your motivations,
　　Take hold of yourself.

Fellow travelers
Make the long journey
        Seem shorter.

        Force and counterforce
Create friction,
        Else nothing would work.

        In other words,
Friction
        Is necessary.

It is neither
Just or unjust,
    Only physics.

Concerts
Awaken our need
    For higher energies.

    Routine is helpful,
As being awake
    Comes in fits and starts.

Pride, even though justified,
Is earthly,
    In scale, relinquished.

    We cannot attribute
To ourselves that which
    Does not belong to us.

    If our job is to learn,
Help others, and evolve,
    What really belongs to us?

Space is an unknown,
But not empty,
Full of wanderers.

Fear of nothingness
Is a lack of awareness
Of one's Self.

Curtain opens,
Take a bow,
It is now, Be.

Your house is on fire!
Don't sit on your hands,
    Rise and fly.

    A galactic speck,
A solar system speck,
    An earth speck, all beloved.

    Indigo depth piercing
Time,
    Riding waves to eternity.

Eternal now
Cresting mountain of
        Past and future tribulations.

    Curtain lowers
On unresolved issues,
        Each evening, dream deep.

    Broken heart
Will mend,
        Broken trust more difficult.

Pursue your interests
With a light heart,
    Essence joys are jewels.

    Making plans and lists
Helps,
    But only if you follow them.

    Don't be afraid
To give a hearty laugh
    At yourself once in a while.

A break in the rain,
Cool clear sky
Breathing sunlight.

Right action
Isn't always
Easily determined.

Decisions
When weighed in balance
Can seem arbitrary.

A pure heart
Can fairly decide
      Most issues.

    Notch your arrow,
Aim high,
      Shoot for the sun.

    Our time-bodies make
Incredible design patterns
      On planet Earth.

If we were large enough,
Planets could be
   Stepping stones.

Solar system's edge
Is a good place to view
   Our galaxy.

A speck in our world
Is a giant
   In the molecular world.

Pure white light
Of Presence
      Pierces the universe.

    Awake, alive, together,
Light from above
      Is our actual home.

    The gift of Presence
Makes all other gifts
      Irrelevant.

Breathing, resting, eating,
Life functions,
Describe the Earth in us.

Divine aims, Love, efforts,
Essence Presence,
Describe the Stars in us.

Each one of us
Salutes the other
With knowing compassion.

We cannot be grateful enough,
For our
        Sublime luck.

    This little soul
Peeks out,
        The world is a scary place.

    We are the Gods' vineyard,
Distillation is only
        For the few ripest ones.

Green apples,
Sour cherries,
        Pucker up and kiss a lot.

    Lemony sunlight
Slanting through shades,
        Drawing floor patterns.

    The baby essence is limp
In my arms,
        Dreams tell some truths.

Feed essence
Refined nourishment,
    Growth is slow, deliberate.

    Spontaneity brightens
A dull day,
    But planning can be good.

    Granular closeness
Can be a bit much,
    But useful for examining self.

Whitewashing,
Good for fences,
Bad for lies.

Being swayed by others
May happen, but
Conscience may complain.

Our rough edges
Are chiseled away
By loving hands.

Finishing is both joy
And sadness, as well as
    Space for something new.

Make a circle
With joined hands,
    Celebrate shared Love.

Nature's perfection
Is exhibited best
    In a beautiful garden.

Rocky, sandy coastlines,
Mounting waves of froth,
  Salt air, rugged beauty.

We are anxious to ascend,
But are naïve
  To the payment required.

Generously give,
For what have you
  To lose?

A humble beginning,
Through to a quiet ending,
Cycle completed.

www.ingramcontent.com/pod-product-compliance
Lightning Source LLC
Chambersburg PA
CBHW031415290426
44110CB00011B/397